TABLE OF CONTENTS

INTRODUCTION

CHAPTER ONE: DO YOU KNOW YOUR BAD HABITS?
- The Sincere Question
- Tackling Bad Habits with Patience and Prioritization
- Navigating the Challenges of Habit Change

CHAPTER TWO: STEPS TO BREAKING BAD HABITS

CHAPTER THREE: 'ABRUPTLY' APPROACH
- Understanding the Abruptly Method
- The advantages of the abrupt approach
- Challenges and Pitfalls
- Success Stories and Lessons Learned
- Building Resilience and Self-Empowerment

CHAPTER FOUR: REWIRING YOUR BRAIN:
- Transforming Habits for a Better You
- The Persistence of Habits: Hardwiring in the Brain
- Overwriting Habits: A Cognitive Approach
- The Importance of Behavioral Reprogramming
- Effective Habit Transformation: The Power of New Patterns
- Practical Application: Substituting Habits for Healthier Choices
- Long-Term Habit Reinforcement: Establishing Lasting Change

INTRODUCTION

We all have habits, both good and bad, that shape our daily lives and impact our ability to achieve our goals. Some of the most problematic habits are quite obvious - things like smoking, excessive drinking, or indulging in too much junk food. These types of unhealthy behaviors are well-known to have detrimental effects on our physical and mental wellbeing. But there is another category of bad habits that can be even more insidious and difficult to recognize.

These are the subtle, ingrained patterns of behavior that we've developed over years, often without even realizing the negative impact they are having. They might be habits that interfere with our productivity and ability to get things done, like a tendency to procrastinate or constantly get distracted. Or they could be social habits that limit our personal and professional relationships, such as shyness, poor communication skills, or an inability to make eye contact. Whatever form they take, these under-the-radar bad habits can quietly but steadily hold us back from living our best lives and achieving our true potential.

The reason these types of habits are so problematic is that we often don't even realize they are problematic. They feel normal, even natural, because they've become such an entrenched part of our daily routines. But over time, they can prevent us from getting the things we really want, whether that's a dream job, a fulfilling relationship, good health, or simply a deeper sense of personal growth and achievement.

The good news is, it is possible to identify and break free from even the most stubbornly embedded bad habits. This report will provide you with 5 proven strategies to help you do just that. Of course, it won't be easy - changing long-standing behaviors and thought patterns requires a serious commitment of time, effort and perseverance. But if you're willing to put in the work, the payoff can be truly transformative.

Imagine how empowered you'll feel when you finally kick that nail-biting habit that's been a source of embarrassment for years. Or picture how your relationships might blossom if you could overcome your shyness and start making more genuine connections with people. And just think of the boost to your productivity and career prospects if you could learn to finally overcome the tendency to procrastinate.

Breaking bad habits isn't a quick or painless process, but the benefits are well worth it. With the right techniques and a steadfast determination, you can absolutely transform the detrimental patterns that have been holding you back. It may take time and sustained effort, but once you do, you'll be amazed at how much freer and more fulfilled you feel. The key is to approach it with an open mind, a patient spirit, and an unwavering commitment to personal growth. If you do, the results can be truly life-changing.

So, get ready to take an honest look at the habits that may be silently sabotaging your success, and learn the strategies to finally break those cycles for good. Your best self is waiting to emerge - all you have to do is put in the work to uncover it.

Chapter

ONE

DO YOU KNOW YOUR BAD HABITS?

Identifying and acknowledging our bad habits can be one of the most challenging personal development tasks we face. Many of our ingrained behaviors and tendencies operate at a subconscious level, deeply rooted in our psyche and often going unnoticed on a day-to-day basis. However, taking the time to truly understand and confront our bad habits is a crucial step towards personal growth and self-improvement.

The good news is that the most effective way to uncover our bad habits is often the simplest - we simply need to ask ourselves directly what they are. This may sound too easy to be impactful, but the power of this approach lies in its ability to tap into the wealth of information stored within our subconscious minds.

Our habits, both good and bad, are fundamentally encoded in the subconscious. It is the repository of our learned behaviors, automatic responses, and deep-seated patterns of thinking and acting. While we may be acutely aware of certain bad habits, such as biting our nails or procrastinating on important tasks, there are likely many more that lurk beneath the surface of our conscious awareness.

The Sincere Question

By posing the question "What are my bad habits?" directly to ourselves, we are activating a powerful mechanism. Our subconscious, when presented with a clear and specific inquiry, will feel compelled to provide us with the answers. It is as if we are shining a spotlight into the depths of our own psyche, illuminating the hidden corners where our less-than-desirable behaviors reside.

The key is to create the right conditions for this self-exploration. Find a quiet, distraction-free environment where you can focus your attention inward. Turn off the television, silence your phone, and remove any other potential sources of interruption. This allows your conscious mind to fully engage with the task at hand, without being pulled in multiple directions.

Once you have set the stage, begin by simply asking yourself the question: "What are my bad habits?" Write down each response that surfaces, without judgment or criticism. It is important to approach this exercise with an open and curious mindset, rather than one of self-criticism or shame.

You may be surprised by the answers that emerge. Some of your bad habits may be quite obvious, while others may be more subtle or deeply ingrained. Perhaps you'll discover that you have a tendency to procrastinate on important tasks, or that you often engage in mindless snacking when feeling stressed. Maybe you'll realize that you have a habit of interrupting others during conversations, or that you struggle to manage your time effectively.

Whatever the revelations, it is crucial that you resist the urge to immediately berate yourself or feel overwhelmed by the list. Remember, the goal of this exercise is not to create a sense of shame or guilt, but rather to empower you with self-knowledge. Armed with this information, you can begin the process of addressing and ultimately breaking these undesirable habits.

It's important to note that the list of bad habits you uncover may be quite extensive. This is not necessarily a cause for concern, but rather a testament to the depth and complexity of our subconscious programming. The human mind is a vast and intricate landscape, with countless pathways and patterns that have been shaped by our experiences, beliefs, and environmental influences.

Tackling Bad Habits with Patience and Prioritization

As you review your list of bad habits, resist the urge to feel overwhelmed or to attempt to tackle them all at once. Instead, approach the process with a sense of compassion and patience. Prioritize the habits that you feel are the most detrimental to your well-being or that are the most feasible to address first. This will help you maintain a sense of focus and prevent you from becoming bogged down in an endless cycle of self-improvement.

Remember, the simple act of acknowledging and identifying your bad habits is a significant accomplishment in itself. By bringing these behaviors to the surface, you are taking the first crucial step towards creating positive change in your life. The path to breaking bad habits may not be a straight or easy one, but with determination, self-compassion, and a willingness to learn and grow, you can absolutely succeed.

As you continue to explore and unpack the bad habits you've uncovered, be mindful of the potential roadblocks and obstacles you may encounter along the way. Change is not always easy, and old habits can be deeply entrenched and resistant to transformation. You may find yourself slipping back into familiar patterns, or experiencing moments of frustration and self-doubt.

Navigating the Challenges of Habit Change
When these challenges arise, it's important to have a toolbox of strategies and techniques to help you navigate them. Consider seeking the support of a therapist, life coach, or trusted friend or family

member who can provide guidance, accountability, and encouragement. Engage in regular self-reflection and journaling to track your progress and identify areas where you may need to adjustyour approach.

Remember, too, that breaking bad habits is not a one-time event, but rather an ongoing process of self-discovery and growth. There will be ups and downs, successes and setbacks, but each step forward is a testament to your resilience and commitment to personal betterment.

As you continue to explore and address your bad habits, also be mindful of the positive habits and behaviors you can cultivate to replace them. What healthy rituals, routines, or mindsets can you adopt to fill the void left by the elimination of your undesirable habits? By approaching this process with a spirit of creativity and experimentation, you can transform not just your bad habits, but your entire way of being.

Ultimately, the journey of uncovering and breaking bad habits is a deeply empowering one. It requires vulnerability, courage, and a willingness to face the darker corners of our psyche. But in doing so, we unlock the potential for profound personal growth, self-mastery, and a deeper connection to our true selves.

So, the next time you find yourself wondering about your bad habits, don't hesitate to ask the question directly. Embrace the simplicity of this approach, and trust that your subconscious will provide you with the answers you seek. With a steadfast commitment to self-exploration and a compassionate, growth-oriented mindset, you can embark on a transformative journey towards a healthier, more fulfilling way of living.

Chapter

TWO

STEPS TO BREAKING BAD HABITS

Each person possesses a mix of good and bad habits. Typically, it's easier for individuals to pinpoint their bad habits rather than their good ones. If you've followed our previous advice, you should have already identified some of your negative habits.

Now, what's the next step? Many individuals express a desire to break free from all their bad habits, yet they struggle to find the most effective approach. They experiment with various methods but find it challenging to permanently eliminate these habits. Even if they make progress, the bad habits often resurface.

The initial step to breaking a bad habit is understanding its nature. Essentially, a habit is a behavior pattern that you frequently repeat, triggered in your subconscious mind. Since both your good and bad habits are deeply ingrained in your subconscious, identifying them can be tricky. This is where the questioning technique for recognizing your bad habits proves to be invaluable.

You are essentially the sum of your habits, both positive and negative. To truly overcome your bad habits, it's crucial to gain insight into how they originated. Contrary to what you might think, this isn't as daunting as it sounds.

The formation of any habit follows a process involving four key components:
1. The trigger
2. The craving
3. The response
4. The reward

When you break down your habits into these four stages, it becomes easier to comprehend how habits function and consequently find a way to break them.

Psychologists refer to this as the "habit loop" – a trigger prompting a craving, leading to a behavior that ultimately provides a reward.

(1) THE TRIGGER

- The trigger is the initial cue or stimulus that prompts the habitual behavior.
- Triggers can be external (e.g., seeing a certain location, hearing a sound, encountering a particular person) or internal (e.g., experiencing a certain emotion, feeling a physical sensation).
- Triggers are the starting point of the habit loop, setting the entire process in motion.
- Understanding your unique triggers is crucial, as it allows you to identify the root cause of your habits and develop strategies to interrupt them.

External Triggers:

External triggers are events, situations, or environmental factors that prompt the habitual behavior.

Examples of external triggers include:

- Seeing a particular location or object (e.g., thc pantry when you want to snack)
- Hearing a specific sound (e.g., the notification sound on your phone)
- Encountering a certain person or social context (e.g., going out with friends who smoke)
- External triggers are often the most obvious and easy to identify, as they are tangible elements in your environment.

Internal Triggers:

Internal triggers are psychological or physiological states that spark the habitual response.

Examples of internal triggers include:

- Experiencing a particular emotion (e.g., feeling stressed, bored, or anxious)

- Having a specific thought or mental state (e.g., ruminating on negative thoughts)
- Experiencing a physical sensation (e.g., feeling hungry, fatigued, or restless)
- Internal triggers can be more subtle and challenging to recognize, as they arise from within the individual.

For instance, a stressful day at work triggers a craving for a drink. Instead of heading straight home, you find yourself at the nearby bar where you spend the evening, signaling pleasure to your brain.

(2) THE CRAVING

The craving is the psychological or physiological desire that emerges in response to the trigger. It is the motivational force that drives you to engage in the habitual behavior.

Cravings are a crucial part of the habit loop because they are what compel us to act, even when we know the behavior may not be in our best interest. Understanding the nature of cravings and how they operate is essential for breaking the hold of bad habits.

1. Psychological Cravings:

- Psychological cravings are the mental and emotional desires that fuel our habitual behaviors.
- These cravings are often rooted in deeper psychological needs, such as a desire for pleasure, stress relief, or a sense of control.
- For example, the psychological craving to check social media might stem from a need for social connection or validation.
- Psychological cravings can be influenced by factors like mood, stress levels, and even social pressures.

2. Physiological Cravings:

- Physiological cravings are the physical, biological desires that drive habitual behaviors.

- These cravings are often triggered by imbalances or changes in the brain's chemistry and neurotransmitter levels.

- For instance, the craving for a sugary snack may be driven by a drop in blood sugar or a spike in insulin levels.

- Physiological cravings can also be influenced by factors like sleep deprivation, hormonal changes, or underlying health conditions.

Cravings can be extremely powerful and compelling, as they tap into our brain's reward and pleasure centers. When we engage in a habitual behavior, our brain releases feel-good chemicals like dopamine, creating a positive feedback loop that reinforces the habit.

To break the habit loop, it's essential to address the underlying craving. This might involve:

- Identifying the root cause of the craving (e.g., the psychological need or physiological imbalance)
- Developing alternative strategies to meet the need or address the imbalance (e.g., finding healthier stress-relief activities)
- Practicing mindfulness and acceptance to observe the craving without acting on it
- Gradually reducing the intensity and frequency of the craving over time

(3) THE RESPONSE

The response is the actual behavior or action taken to satisfy the craving. This is the habit itself - the ingrained pattern of behavior that has become automatic and difficult to break.

Responses can take on many forms, both physical and mental:

1. **Physical Responses:**

- These are the overt, observable actions that make up the habitual behavior.

- Examples of physical responses include:

- Biting nails

- Smoking a cigarette

- Mindlessly scrolling through social media

- Snacking on unhealthy foods

- Physical responses are often the most visible and tangible aspect of a habit, and they can have direct consequences on our physical health and well-being.

2. Mental Responses:

- These are the internal, cognitive patterns that constitute the habitual behavior.

- Examples of mental responses include:

- Ruminating on negative thoughts

- Engaging in excessive worrying

- Procrastinating on important tasks

- Engaging in compulsive mental rituals

- Mental responses can be just as ingrained and difficult to break as physical habits, as they are deeply wired into our thought processes and patterns of thinking.

The response is the culmination of the habit loop, where the craving is acted upon and the behavior is reinforced. It is the habit itself - the automatic, almost unconscious way in which we react to the trigger.

Overcoming the response is a critical step in breaking the habit loop. This typically involves:

1. Identifying the specific response: Clearly understanding the exact behavior or thought pattern that makes up the habit.
2. Interrupting the response: Developing strategies to disrupt the automatic nature of the response, such as replacing it with an alternative behavior or consciously redirecting attention.

3. Replacing the response: Substituting the problematic response with a more positive, healthy alternative that still meets the underlying need or craving.

4. Reinforcing the new response: Consistently practicing the new, desired behavior until it becomes the new automatic response.

(4) THE REWARD

The reward is the positive outcome or consequence that reinforces the habitual behavior, leading to the habit loop being repeated. Rewards can take many forms, both tangible and intangible:

1. Tangible Rewards:

- These are the physical or material benefits that come from engaging in the habitual behavior.
- Examples of tangible rewards include:
- The immediate pleasure or satisfaction of consuming a sugary snack

- The feeling of relaxation after smoking a cigarette
- The dopamine rush from receiving a "like" on a social media post
- Tangible rewards provide a clear, measurable payoff that can make the habit feel irresistible in the moment.

2. Intangible Rewards:
- These are the psychological, emotional, or social benefits that reinforce the habitual behavior.
- Examples of intangible rewards include:
- The sense of comfort or escape from negative emotions when engaging in a compulsive behavior
- The feeling of social connection or belonging when participating in a group habit
- The sense of accomplishment or control when completing a habitual task

- Intangible rewards can be more subtle and subjective, but they can be just as powerful in driving and maintaining habitual behaviors.

The reward is a crucial component of the habit loop because it provides the positive reinforcement that encourages the brain to repeat the behavior. Each time you engage in the habit and experience the reward, the connection between the trigger, craving, and response becomes stronger, making the habit harder to break.

To disrupt the habit loop, it's important to address the reward component. This may involve:

1. Identifying the specific reward you're seeking and finding alternative ways to meet that need.
2. Delaying or modifying the reward to reduce its immediate gratification.
3. Introducing new, more positive rewards that align with your desired goals and values.

4. Gradually decreasing the reward over time to
    weaken the habit's hold.

These four elements form a neurological loop that allows you to establish new habits and run them automatically. Once triggered, the routine is followed almost instinctively, though it's not entirely automatic; it just happens swiftly. Fortunately, there are several effective methods to eradicate bad habits from your life, and some may work better for you based on your individual tendencies and circumstances.

In subsequent chapters we will see the five most common strategies to breaking negative habits.

Chapter

THREE

'ABRUPTLY' APPROACH

Eliminating undesirable habits is a common pursuit for many individuals seeking personal growth and self-improvement. One method that has been widely recognized for its effectiveness, albeit its challenges, is the "abruptly" approach. This technique involves making a decisive and immediate break from a habit, whether it be smoking, overeating, or excessive screen time. While this method can yield positive results, it also presents unique obstacles that individuals must navigate on their journey to behavioral change.

Understanding the Abruptly Method

The concept of going abruptly, involves a radical departure from a habit without gradual reduction or easing. For instance, if someone is trying to quit smoking abruptly, they would stop smoking entirely from a specific moment forward. This approach is often associated with swift and decisive action, aiming to cut off the habit at its root.

The advantages of the abrupt approach

The advantages of the abrupt approach are numerous:

- Decisiveness and commitment: By taking a firm, all-or-nothing stance, the individual demonstrates a strong commitment to change and a willingness to make a decisive break from the habit. This level of commitment can be a powerful motivator for change.

- Avoiding gradual relapse: Gradual reduction methods can sometimes lead to a gradual relapse, as the individual may slowly revert to the old behavior. The abrupt approach aims to prevent this by not allowing any "slips" or gradual reintroduction of the habit.

- Psychological impact: The abrupt approach can have a powerful psychological impact, as the individual experiences a clear, unambiguous shift in their behavior. This can create a sense of momentum and a renewed determination to maintain the change, as the individual feels they have crossed a significant threshold.

- Disruptive nature: The abrupt approach is inherently disruptive to the existing habit loop. By severing the connections between the trigger, craving, and response all at once, the individual forces their brain to adapt to a new reality, paving the way for the establishment of a new, healthier habit.

- Clarity and focus: With the habit eliminated entirely, the individual can direct their energy and attention towards developing alternative, more beneficial behaviors, without the distraction or temptation of the old habit.

Challenges and Pitfalls

While the abruptly method can be effective for some individuals, it comes with its own set of challenges. One of the primary difficulties is the abrupt change in routine and behavior, which can trigger withdrawal symptoms or intense cravings. These challenges may test an individual's willpower and resilience, leading to potential relapses if not managed effectively.

Moreover, the sudden cessation of a habit can disrupt established patterns and coping mechanisms, leaving individuals vulnerable to stress and emotional turmoil. This adjustment period can be emotionally taxing and may require additional support systems or coping strategies to navigate successfully.

Success Stories and Lessons Learned

Despite the challenges associated with the abruptly method, many individuals have successfully overcome their bad habits through sheer determination and commitment. These success stories serve as a testament to the power of willpower and the human capacity for change.

One key lesson learned from adopting the abruptly approach is the importance of mindset and determination in achieving behavioral change. By setting clear goals, establishing a support system, and staying committed to the process, individuals can increase their likelihood of success in breaking bad habits.

Building Resilience and Self-Empowerment

Breaking a bad habit using the abruptly method can have profound effects on an individual's sense of self-efficacy and empowerment. By demonstrating the ability to make significant changes in their behavior, individuals strengthen their belief in their capacity to overcome challenges and adversity in other areas of their lives.

When an individual decides to break a bad habit using the abrupt method, they are taking a bold and decisive step that can have far-reaching effects on their overall well-being and self-perception.

1. Strengthening Self-Efficacy:

- By demonstrating the ability to make a significant behavioral change, individuals reinforce their belief in their own capacity to overcome challenges and adversity.

- This sense of self-efficacy, or the belief in one's ability to succeed, is a crucial component of personal empowerment and resilience.

- With each successful abrupt break from a habit, the individual's confidence in their ability to effect change and shape their own future grows stronger.

2. Developing Valuable Qualities:

- The process of breaking a habit abruptly requires the cultivation of valuable qualities such as discipline, perseverance, and self-control.

- Individuals who are able to push through the initial discomfort and cravings associated with an abrupt habit change demonstrate their capacity for self-regulation and determination.

- These qualities can serve individuals well in facing future obstacles and achieving their long-term goals, both in the context of habit change and in other areas of their lives.

3. Fostering a Sense of Empowerment:

- The abrupt approach to habit breaking can instill a powerful sense of empowerment within the individual.

- By taking decisive action and breaking free from a deeply ingrained behavior, the individual gains a tangible sense of control over their own life and choices.

- This feeling of empowerment can be transformative, as it enables the individual to approach other challenges and goals with a renewed sense of agency and confidence.

4. Enhancing Resilience:

- The ability to successfully navigate the challenges and discomfort of an abrupt habit change can build an individual's resilience, or their capacity to bounce back from adversity.

- Overcoming the initial difficulty of an abrupt habit break can equip the individual with the tools and mindset to tackle future obstacles with greater ease and determination.

- Resilience is a valuable asset that can help individuals navigate the ups and downs of life with greater adaptability and emotional stability.

By empowering individuals to make significant behavioral changes and cultivate valuable personal qualities, the abrupt approach to habit breaking can have a profound and lasting impact on an individual's sense of self-efficacy, empowerment, and resilience. These positive outcomes can then extend beyond the realm of habit change, benefiting the individual's overall well-being and ability to achieve their long-term goals.

Moreover, the process of breaking a habit abruptly can instill valuable lessons in discipline, perseverance, and self-control. These qualities can serve individuals well in facing future obstacles and achieving their long-term goals.

Chapter

FOUR

REWIRING YOUR BRAIN:

Transforming Habits for a Better You

Numerous studies have shed light on how the brain stores habits differently compared to other types of memories. When it comes to habits, there is a significant emotional component that acts as a trigger, leading to strong urges to engage in specific behaviors. This mechanism highlights the intricate relationship between emotions, triggers, and habitual actions.

Habits are deeply ingrained behaviors that our brains have automated, allowing us to carry out routine tasks without conscious thought. This frees up our cognitive resources to focus on other matters, like planning meals.

However, the brain's executive control center does not relinquish complete authority over habitual behaviors. A recent study by Massachusetts' neuroscientists has found that a specific region of the prefrontal cortex, which is involved in higher-order thinking and planning, maintains a level of moment-to-moment control over which habits are activated at any given time.

The benefit of habits is that they don't require conscious deliberation, liberating the brain to attend to other concerns. "However, it doesn't free up all of it. There's some piece of your cortex that's still devotedto that control."

In essence, while habits automate many of our routine actions, the brain's executive functions still retain a degree of oversight and regulation over these ingrained behavioral patterns.

The findings indicate that the infralimbic (IL) cortex is responsible for determining, moment-to-moment, which habitual behaviors will be expressed.

The Persistence of Habits: Hardwiring in the Brain

One school of thought suggests that habits become hardwired in the brain once they are formed. According to this perspective, once a habit is established, it becomes a permanent fixture in one's behavioral repertoire. This notion implies that attempting to eliminate a habit entirely may be an insurmountable challenge, leading to the belief that individuals may carry these habits for the rest of their lives. This theory could potentially explain the high rates of relapse seen in individuals recovering from addiction, as the ingrained nature of habits may make breaking free a formidable task.

Overwriting Habits: A Cognitive Approach

In contrast to the traditional view of habits as permanently hardwired, an alternative perspective proposes a more dynamic approach to habit change. Rather than simply trying to eliminate or erase an entrenched "bad" habit, this view suggests actively overwriting it with a new, healthier routine.

Consciously substitute the old, undesirable behavior with a positive alternative when the habitual trigger is encountered. By replacing the former habit with a constructive response, individuals can effectively "rewire" their brains to adopt a different pattern of behavior.

This dynamic approach harnesses the brain's remarkable neuroplasticity - its ability to reorganize and adapt its neural connections in response to new experiences. Instead of seeing habits as immutable, this view recognizes the potential to reshape them over time through conscious effort and reinforcement.

Rather than resigning themselves to the grip of bad habits, people can take an active role in establishing new, beneficial routines. By consistently substituting the old habit with a replacement behavior, the brain gradually adapts, and the new pattern becomes the dominant response.

This dynamic perspective offers a more empowering alternative to the notion of habits as permanently hardwired and resistant to change. It suggests that with the right techniques, individuals can actively rewire their brains and replace entrenched habits with healthier alternatives.

The Importance of Behavioral Reprogramming
To successfully overwrite a habit, the new routine must be compelling and potent enough to replace the existing behavior. This concept is rooted in the

principles of neuro-linguistic programming (NLP), a methodology that focuses on restructuring thought patterns and behaviors to achieve desired outcomes. NLP techniques aim to interrupt negative or destructive habits and replace them with more constructive and beneficial ones.

Effective Habit Transformation: The Power of New Patterns

Implementing this approach involves transforming the existing habit loop by introducing a new, more meaningful pattern of behavior. By replacing the original habit loop with one that holds greater significance or reward, individuals can create a positive feedback loop that reinforces the new behavior. This process of consciously reshaping habits aligns with personal values and goals, facilitating long-term behavioral change.

Practical Application: Substituting Habits for Healthier Choices

An illustrative example of habit substitution involves addressing smoking behavior. When faced with the urge to smoke, individuals can choose to replace this detrimental habit with a healthier alternative, such as engaging in gentle exercise. By consciously prioritizing their health over the temporary pleasure derived from smoking, individuals can establish a new, health-promoting routine that gradually supplants the old habit.

Long-Term Habit Reinforcement: Establishing Lasting Change

Consistency and persistence are key to solidifying new habits and minimizing the likelihood of reverting to old patterns. Over time, repeatedly engaging in the new behavior reinforces neural pathways associated with the preferred habit, making it increasingly challenging to return to the previous undesirable behavior. By prioritizing self-care, health, and well-being, individuals can cultivate lasting changes that promote overall wellness and personal growth.

Understanding the intricacies of habit formation in the brain and exploring effective strategies for habit change can empower individuals to break free from detrimental behaviors and cultivate positive habits. By leveraging cognitive approaches, behavioral reprogramming techniques, and the reinforcement of new patterns, individuals can navigate the complexities of habit transformation with intentionality and determination. Through conscious effort and a commitment to personal growth, individuals can overwrite old habits with healthier alternatives, leading to lasting change and enhanced well-being.

Chapter

FIVE

GRADUAL PROGRESSION APPROACH:
A Balanced Method for Habit Transformation

While the two previous perspectives on habit change offer valuable insights, a hybrid "Gradual Progression Approach" combines elements of both to provide a balanced, realistic strategy for transforming entrenched behaviors.

The Gradual Progression Approach acknowledges that for many people, the prospect of abruptly and completely eliminating a deeply ingrained habit may not be a viable or sustainable solution. Habits, by their very nature, are deeply woven into our daily routines and psychological patterns. Expecting to simply snap one's fingers and erase a long-standing habit overnight is often an unrealistic expectation.

At the same time, the Gradual Progression Approach recognizes the limitations of the dynamic habit change perspective. While consciously replacing an old habit with a new routine is a powerful technique, it still requires a significant degree of conscious effort and willpower to implement consistently over an extended period.

The Gradual Progression Approach, therefore, offers a middle ground - a structured framework for incrementally modifying habit patterns over time. Instead of demanding an immediate, wholesale shift, this method encourages individuals to take a more paced, step-by-step approach to habit transformation.

The process might involve gradually reducing the frequency or duration of the undesirable habit, while simultaneously building up the new, replacement behavior in parallel. For example, someone trying to break a smoking habit could start by cutting back from a pack a day to half a pack, while also establishing a new routine of taking a brief walk break instead of lighting up.

Over time, as the new habit becomes more ingrained, the individual can continue to dial back the old behavior until it is fully replaced. This gradual, progressive approach tends to be more sustainable than abrupt cessation, as it does not rely solely on willpower and allows the brain to adapt to the changes at a manageable pace.

Ultimately, the Gradual Progression Approach offers a compromise - a balanced method that harnesses the insights of both previous perspectives to provide a viable path for transforming deeply entrenched habits. By combining elements of both approaches, it enables individuals to break free from detrimental behaviors through a structured, step-by-step process.

Analyzing Triggers and Implementing Small Changes

The key to the Gradual Progression Approach lies in closely examining the triggers and contextual factors associated with the undesirable habit, and then systematically implementing small, incremental changes to disrupt that behavioral pattern.

The first crucial step is for individuals to become acutely aware of the specific situations, emotions, or environmental cues that tend to precede their engagement in the bad habit. Whether it's reaching for a cigarette after a stressful meeting, mindlessly snacking while watching TV, or procrastinating on work during certain times of day - identifying these trigger points is essential.

Once the triggers have been clearly mapped out, the next phase involves gradually reducing or modifying the individual's response to those triggers. Rather than attempting to eliminate the habit cold turkey, the Gradual Progression Approach advocates for slowly dialing back the behavior through a series of small, manageable changes.

For example, someone trying to quit smoking might start by committing to smoke one fewer cigarette per day. Over time, they can continue to incrementally decrease their daily consumption, all the while building up replacement behaviors like taking a short walk or engaging in deep breathing exercises when the urge to smoke arises.

Similarly, an individual attempting to break a habit of stress-eating might begin by limiting their unhealthy snacking to specific times of day, rather than allowing it throughout the entire evening. They could then gradually extend the "snack-free" periods, while simultaneously stocking the kitchen with healthier alternatives and developing new stress management techniques.

The beauty of this approach lies in its sensitivity to human nature and the brain's natural resistance to dramatic, overnight changes. By breaking the habit transformation process into tiny, achievable steps, individuals are less likely to become overwhelmed or rapidly revert to their old behaviors. Each small win builds momentum and reinforces the new neural pathways, eventually leading to the replacement of the undesirable habit.

Patience and consistency are key, as is a willingness to occasionally stumble and recommit. But through this methodical, trigger-focused strategy, people can steadily rewrite their entrenched habits and establish healthier, more beneficial patterns of behavior.

Implementing Weekly Reduction Goals

A recommended approach is to set weekly reduction goals, such as decreasing the daily consumption of cigarettes by one increment each week. By adhering to this structured timeline, individuals are compelled to strive towards achieving the next milestone, fostering a sense of progress and accomplishment. Consistent adherence to these incremental changes can ultimately lead to the eradication of the habit altogether.

Adapting the Method to Various Habits

The Gradual Progression Approach can be applied to a wide range of habits, including reducing candy intake, moderating alcohol consumption, and addressing other detrimental behaviors. By quantifying the frequency of the habit and gradually decreasing engagement over time, individuals can effectively curtail their reliance on these behaviors.

Embracing Imperfection and Maintaining Resilience

One of the key tenets of the Gradual Progression Approach is the recognition that habit change, despite its incremental nature, is rarely a linear process. Inevitably, individuals attempting to modify deeply ingrained behaviors will encounter occasional setbacks and moments of relapse. Acknowledging and embracing this reality is essential for maintaining the resilience and self-compassion required for long-term success.

Rather than berating themselves or viewing any deviation from the plan as a complete failure, proponents of the Gradual Progression Approach encourage individuals to approach such slip-ups with understanding and kindness. The simple fact is that habits, by their very nature, are deeply rooted in the brain's neural pathways and automatic responses.

Undoing these well-trodden patterns takes time, effort, and a willingness to occasionally stumble.

Avoid getting mired in self-criticism or allowing a single lapse to derail the entire process. When faced with a momentary relapse, individuals should take a step back, reflect on the underlying triggers or circumstances that contributed to the setback, and then refocus their attention on resuming the new, healthier routine the following day.

This approach fosters a mindset of persistence and self-compassion, which are vital for sustaining the gradual habit transformation process. Beating oneself up over a momentary lapse or indulgence in the old behavior only serves to undermine motivation and resilience. Instead, by acknowledging their humanity and treating themselves with kindness, individuals can more effectively recommit to their goals and continue making steady progress.

Ultimately, the Gradual Progression Approach recognizes that perfection is neither achievable nor necessary for successful habit change. What matters most is maintaining an unwavering commitment to the overarching objective, while also extending grace and understanding to oneself throughout the inevitable ups and downs of the journey.

By embracing imperfection and responding to setbacks with resilience, individuals can navigate the habit transformation process with a more balanced, sustainable mindset. This, in turn, increases the likelihood of establishing lasting, beneficial behavioral patterns that truly take root and become integrated into one's daily life.

Cultivating Discipline and Persistence

While the Gradual Progression Approach is not without its challenges, it has demonstrated efficacy in facilitating habit change for many individuals. Success with this approach hinges on the cultivation of discipline and persistence, qualities that can benefit personal growth beyond the realm of habit transformation. By committing to incremental progress and maintaining a proactive mindset, individuals can navigate the journey towards breaking free from detrimental habits with determination and resilience.

Chapter

SIX

Redirecting Focus: A Shift in Approach

Rather than fixating on the negative aspects of their behavior, individuals seeking to break a detrimental habit can find greater success by shifting their focus and energy towards more positive, constructive alternatives. This redirected approach helps to minimize feelings of restriction and deprivation that can often undermine habit change efforts.

The core premise of this strategy is to actively divert attention away from the unwanted behavior and consciously channel it towards more desirable activities and lifestyle choices. Instead of constantly dwelling on the habit they are trying to break, individuals are encouraged to cultivate a mindset of abundance, where they direct their focus and resources towards building new, healthier patterns.

For example, someone trying to overcome a dependence on social media might make a concerted effort to engage in more face-to-face interactions, pursue hobbies and interests outside of the digital realm, or dedicate time to learning a new skill. By immersing themselves in these enriching alternatives, they can gradually diminish the psychological and emotional pull of the habit they are attempting to break.

Similarly, an individual struggling with unhealthy eating habits might shift their focus towards discovering nourishing, delicious recipes, experimenting with new ingredients, and finding joy in the act of preparing and sharing meals with loved ones. This shift in mindset can make the prospect of giving up unhealthy snacks or fast food feel less like a deprivation and more like an opportunity to cultivate a richer, more fulfilling relationship with food.

The beauty of this redirected approach lies in its ability to reframe the habit change process. Rather than viewing it as a constant struggle against an unwanted behavior, individuals can instead embrace it as a chance to explore new possibilities and expand their horizons. This sense of exploration and growth can foster a greater sense of intrinsic motivation and long-term sustainability, as the new, positive habits become integrated into one's daily life.

Of course, this is not to say that the individual can entirely ignore the habit they are trying to break. Maintaining some degree of awareness and monitoring of the undesirable behavior is still necessary. But by purposefully shifting their focus and energy towards constructive alternatives, they can significantly diminish the power and appeal of the detrimental habit, paving the way for lasting, meaningful change.

Overcoming Pleasure Temptation

When individuals are accustomed to deriving pleasure or comfort from a habit, such as consuming multiple beers daily, the prospect of relinquishing this source of gratification can be daunting. The allure of the pleasurable sensation associated with the habit can intensify the challenge of breaking free from it.

Balancing Attention: The Pitfalls of Fixation

Constantly fixating on eliminating a bad habit can consume a significant portion of one's daily thoughts and actions, fostering a sense of deprivation and restraint. This heightened focus on restriction may lead individuals to perceive the change as a loss of a long-standing source of enjoyment, reinforcing the belief that habits, whether positive or negative, define one's identity.

Rational Understanding vs. Emotional Attachments

When it comes to breaking a detrimental habit, individuals often find themselves in a complex and paradoxical situation. On one hand, they may have a rational, intellectual understanding of the negative impacts the habit has on their health, well-being, and overall quality of life. The data, statistics, and expert opinions may all clearly point to the necessity of cessation. Yet, on the other hand, they often find themselves grappling with deep-seated emotional attachments and coping mechanisms that have become intricately linked to the very behavior they know they should abandon.

This disconnect between the rational mind and the emotional heart can prove to be a significant hurdle in the habit change process. The rational understanding may underscore the importance of letting go of the habit, but the emotional allure and perceived benefits it once provided can make that task immensely challenging.

For example, someone struggling with a smoking habit may intellectually acknowledge the well-documented health risks and financial burdens associated with the addiction. They may have a clear, rational grasp of the necessity of quitting. Yet, the ritual of lighting a cigarette, the sensory experience, and the perceived stress-relieving properties of the habit can create a powerful emotional attachment that is far more difficult to sever.

Similarly, an individual trying to break an unhealthy eating pattern may rationally understand the detrimental impact on their physical and mental health, but the comfort, pleasure, and coping mechanisms they have associated with certain foods can make the prospect of change feel daunting and unpalatable.

Navigating this divide between rational understanding and emotional attachment requires a multifaceted approach. It involves not only acknowledging the habit's adverse effects, but also delving into the deeper psychological and emotional factors that have contributed to its persistence. By exploring the underlying needs, triggers, and coping mechanisms that the habit has fulfilled, individuals can begin to cultivate alternative, healthier strategies to address those deeper issues.

Ultimately, the path to breaking a detrimental habit lies in reconciling the rational and the emotional, and finding ways to replace the perceived benefits of the old behavior with more constructive, sustainable alternatives. It is a journey that requires patience, self-compassion, and a willingness to confront the complex interplay between the mind and the heart.

Embracing New Horizons

When individuals find themselves caught between the rational understanding of a habit's detrimental effects and the emotional attachments that have formed around it, a powerful strategy can be to shift the focus from solely eliminating the unwanted behavior to cultivating new, enriching activities and habits. This approach allows them to gradually replace the void left by the relinquished behavior with constructive alternatives that can enhance various aspects of their lives.

Rather than dwelling solely on the habit they are trying to break, this mindset encourages them to explore new horizons and discover activities that align with their values, interests, and aspirations. By dedicating time and energy towards developing positive habits, they can start to build a fulfilling lifestyle that diminishes the psychological and emotional pull of the detrimental behavior.

For instance, someone seeking to overcome a sedentary lifestyle and unhealthy eating habits might begin to explore various forms of physical activity that they find genuinely enjoyable, such as hiking, dancing, or joining a sports league. As they immerse themselves in these new pursuits, they not only improve their physical health but also experience a sense of accomplishment, community, and personal growth that can help offset the perceived benefits of the old, unhealthy habits.

Similarly, an individual struggling with a social media addiction might purposefully cultivate new hobbies and interests that engage them in the physical world, such as learning a musical instrument, volunteering in their community, or taking up a craft or art form. By investing time and energy into these enriching activities, they can gradually replace the habit of compulsively checking their devices with a more meaningful and fulfilling use of their time and attention.

The beauty of this approach lies in its ability to reframe the habit change process from a sense of deprivation to one of expansion and personal growth. Rather than solely focusing on what they are giving up, individuals can direct their focus towards the new horizons they are opening up, the skills they are developing, and the fulfillment they are experiencing in their lives.

This shift in mindset can foster a greater sense of intrinsic motivation and long-term sustainability, as the new, positive habits become integrated into one's daily routine. By embracing new horizons and continuously expanding their repertoire of constructive activities, individuals can gradually diminish the power and appeal of the detrimental habit, paving the way for lasting, meaningful change.

Nurturing Empowering Habits and Building a Foundation for Change

This redirection of focus towards nurturing empowering habits not only fosters personal growth but also diminishes the preoccupation with the negative aspects of one's current lifestyle. While this method has shown effectiveness in facilitating positive change, vigilance is essential to prevent the resurgence of old habits, underscoring the ongoing need to prioritize and reinforce the newly established empowering behaviors.

Chapter

SEVEN

PROGRESS TRACKING AND CELEBRATING MILESTONES

In navigating the journey of breaking detrimental habits, the practice of monitoring progress stands out as a cornerstone for success. While not always deemed a traditional method, its profound impact on sustaining motivation makes it indispensable in the pursuit of positive change. Consider the analogy of the "small steps" approach, where gradual reduction in daily cigarette consumption signifies a commitment to change. Tracking this progress, such as transitioning from 20 to 19 cigarettes daily, not only reinforces discipline but also cultivates a sense of achievement that propels individuals towards further improvement. Achieving and maintaining a reduced cigarette intake, like reaching 19 cigarettes a day for a week, instills a profound sense of pride. This accomplishment serves as a potent motivator, inspiring individuals to persist in their efforts and set their sights on further progress, such as reducing consumption to 18 cigarettes per day.

Reinforcing Positive Habits and Accountability
For those opting for the replacement habit loop method, meticulous tracking of what works and what does not is essential for success. By identifying and amplifying successful strategies, individuals strengthen the foundation of their new habits, gradually replacing old patterns with healthier alternatives. At the core of habit transformation lies a deep commitment to break away from detrimental behaviors. Regularly evaluating adherence to chosen strategies serves as a vital checkpoint, ensuring individuals remain accountable and stay on course towards their goals.

Embracing Abruptly Approach and Personal Triumph

For those bold enough to confront habits head-on by going "Abruptly," daily vigilance becomes paramount. Each day abstained from the habit warrants celebration, fostering a profound sense of accomplishment and fortifying one's resolve to persist in the face of challenges. Imagine a scenario where a daily smoker breaks free from this routine for the first time. This remarkable achievement deserves recognition and celebration, serving as a testament to one's resilience and determination. By visibly tracking each successful day of resistance, individuals witness the gradual accumulation of victories, reinforcing their commitment to change.

Shifting Focus and Daily Reflection

Success in breaking or reinforcing habits often hinges on a shift in focus. By redirecting attention from the immediate pleasures of a habit to the liberation and empowerment that breaking it brings, individuals cultivate a new perspective that fuels their determination and resolve. Consistent monitoring of progress each day serves as a powerful tool in reinforcing positive behaviors and sustaining momentum towards lasting change.

Individuals who embrace this practice, not only track their journey but also celebrate each step taken towards a healthier, more fulfilling lifestyle.

CONCLUSION

The chapters in this book stand as a beacon of hope and a roadmap to personal transformation. Throughout this journey, we have delved into the intricacies of habit formation, understanding the deep-seated mechanisms that drive our behaviors. By exploring the five proven steps meticulously laid out in these pages, you have equipped yourself with the tools necessary to break free from the shackles of negative habits and embrace a life of purpose and fulfillment.

As you reflect on the insights shared within these chapters, remember that change is a gradual process, one that requires patience, dedication, and self-compassion. Celebrate each small victory along the way, for it is these incremental triumphs that pave the path to lasting transformation. Whether you are striving to overcome addiction, procrastination, or any other detrimental behavior, know that you possess the resilience and strength needed to rewrite your story.

As you continue to implement the strategies outlined in this book, keep in mind that setbacks are a natural part of the journey. Embrace these moments as opportunities for growth and learning, reaffirming your commitment to personal development. Surround yourself with a supportive community, seek guidance when needed, and never underestimate the power of self-reflection.

I urge you to embark on this transformative journey with courage and conviction. Trust in your ability to effect change, for within you lies the potential for remarkable growth and renewal. Embrace the challenges that lie ahead as stepping stones towards a brighter, more empowered future. May the lessons learned within these pages serve as a guiding light, illuminating your path to a life filled with purpose, resilience, and joy.